# THE POWER OF YOUR PRESENCE

ALAN SEALE

# THE
# POWER
## OF YOUR
# PRESENCE

*A Daily Workout For Your Soul*

Center for Transformational Presence
PO Box 18471
Rochester, NY 14618

ISBN: 978-0-9825330-1-7

PRINTED IN THE UNITED STATES OF AMERICA

# Table of Contents

# Introduction

*The Power of Your Presence* is a guided meditation in a book—an inner workout designed to lead you step-by-step to your true and authentic presence. The simplicity of the page layout will support your mind to be focused and clear, your heart open and spacious. Lingering for a bit on each page, focusing on your breath and your inner experience, will deepen your awareness and call forth your authentic presence of being. The more you live in your full authentic presence, the greater gift you are to your world.

I invite you to make the *The Power of Your Presence* a part of your daily practice. As you become familiar with the process, you will find your own rhythm and tempo. Let this little book become a good friend—your personal guide to reaching the fullness of *your* authentic presence of being. Give yourself this gift, and you and those whose lives you touch will benefit greatly from the power of your presence.

Many blessings,
Alan Seale

# Presence of Being

What if you could reach a place inside of you
that, when you spoke from that place,
made decisions from that place,
lived from that place,
you were truly in your greatest power?

Not Big Bad Wolf power.
Power to be.  A power of presence.
Your unique presence of being.
Confident and authentic.
Wise and peaceful.

Power to make clear choices.
Power to design and create your greatest life.
Power to move mountains and love deeply.
Power to call forth the best from yourself and others.
Power to transform.

What if you could find that place?
What if you could live there all the time?

How would your career or work change?
How would your relationships change—
with your friends, your family,
your partner or spouse, your colleagues,
even with yourself?
How might your whole world transform?

We can go there now if you would like.
I can be your partner and guide.

All it takes is a few minutes of focused attention each day.
I'll show you the way.

I call it the Presence of Being Workout.
No special gear is required.
Just you and me.

Are you ready?
Then let's go.

# The

# Presence of Being

# Workout

Your Presence of Being Workout begins here.
Turn the pages slowly, giving yourself time
to reflect with each page.

Take a long, slow, deep breath.

Now take an even longer, slower, deeper breath.

Imagine your breath
coming in through your chest,
filling your whole body,
and flowing out through your solar plexus.

Breathe again, even slower.

Let go of any expectations
or preconceived notions
of what should happen
or what you should experience.

Just feel your breath getting deeper.

Let your breath find its own natural, steady rhythm.

Take plenty of time before you turn the page.

Notice how your awareness
is focusing more inward now.

What are you feeling?

Keep breathing . . .
in through your chest,
filling your body,
out through your solar plexus.

Now imagine your soul,
the essence of you,
floating out in front of you.
Close your eyes for a moment if that helps.

Feel its presence—the presence of your soul.

Notice how it shows itself to you.
Perhaps it has a shape or a form.

Perhaps it has a color or texture.

Perhaps it has a sound.

Perhaps a fragrance or taste.

What words describe your soul?

Take a few more moments
to be fully present with your soul.

Ask your soul to tell you
about its greatest strength.

Ask your soul what it wants more of from you.

Now imagine your soul
floating back into your body.

Notice where it lands inside you—
where it settles.

Breathe into that place—
slow, deep, full breaths.

Notice how it feels
to breathe into your soul.

Perhaps emotions come to the surface.

Perhaps it feels calm and peaceful.
Perhaps it feels strong and powerful.

Perhaps it feels uncomfortable
because it's new.

There is no right or wrong feeling.
Just notice
and be willing to stay here
for a few moments.

Keep breathing—
deep, full.

Let your breath
keep finding its own
natural, steady, even rhythm.

Now bring to your awareness
your happiest memory.
Notice where you feel that memory
in your body.

Breathe.

Become aware of
your greatest disappointment.
Where does it live within you?

Breathe.

Become aware of your deepest love.
Where does it live within you?

Breathe.

What has been your greatest loss?
Where in your body do you feel that loss?

Breathe.

Notice where you feel
your greatest power and strength.

Breathe.

Notice where you feel
your greatest fear.

Breathe.

Notice where you feel
your greatest courage.

Breathe.

Notice where you feel
the real you—
authentic and true.

Breathe.

All of these parts
Make up the whole,
authentic you.

Welcome home.

Welcome home to your authentic presence of being.

Take some time to be here.

Just breathe
and get used to
your authentic presence of being.

Who are you?

Why are you here?

Now from your authentic presence of being,
begin to turn your awareness
back out to the world.

Keep breathing
into your authentic presence of being
and consider the events of your day.

Consider situations or challenges.
What do you know about them
from your authentic presence of being?

Breathe again—
authentic presence of being.

Consider your relationships
in which there is great love—
intimates, family, friends, colleagues.

Who in particular comes to mind?

In your authentic presence of being,
what do you bring
to these relationships?

Consider your relationships
in which there is conflict or challenge.

From your authentic presence of being,
what do you know about this conflict or challenge
and its resolution or healing?

Breathe again—
authentic presence of being.

Consider the upcoming events in your life.

What are the opportunities available
in those events if you approach them
from your authentic presence of being?

What if you choose to be
your authentic self in those events?

What difference would it make?

Breathe.

And again.

Presence of being.

When you are in
your authentic presence of being,
you are anchored in your soul.

And it is through your soul
that you access your greatest wisdom,
power, courage, creativity, and strength.

Memorize this feeling.

Claim it as your personal default setting for life.

Meet your day from this place—
your authentic presence of being.

And tomorrow,
repeat this Presence of Being Workout.

From here you can create
your extraordinary life.

From here you can give
your greatest gifts
to those you love
and to the world.

Breathe.

Now go about your day
in your true, authentic, powerful
Presence of Being.

Many blessings.

***The Power of Presence Workout***
is also available as an audio program.
Visit the Center for Transformational Presence
website at
www.transformationalpresence.org.


## The Center for Transformational Presence<sup>SM</sup>

The Center for Transformational Presence<sup>SM</sup> is a discovery, learning, development, and transformation environment for individuals and organizations who are committed to making a significant difference in their world. The Center offers personal coaching as well as courses and training programs in Transformational Leadership, Transformational Presence<sup>SM</sup> Coaching, clarifying your life purpose or soul mission, principles of manifestation, and personal presence.

Through the Center's programs, participants take their next steps in development as transformation agents. As each individual and organization claims the gifts they are here to share, steps fully into living those gifts, and supports others to do the same, together we are able to serve the greater good at all levels of society—family, community, regional, national, multi-national, and global.

To learn more, visit www.transformationalpresence.org.

# Alan Seale

Alan Seale is an award-winning author, inspirational speaker, leadership and transformation coach, and the founder and director of the Center for Transformational Presence[SM]. In addition to ongoing workshops throughout North America and Europe and his work as the principal teacher of the Center for Transformational Presence[SM], Alan currently serves as a guest faculty member of The Graduate Institute in Connecticut and on the coaching faculty of Lobii. As a coach, he serves a full roster of clients from around the world who are committed to bringing extraordinary gifts to the world.

Visit Alan at www.alanseale.com and
www.transformationalpresence.org.

# Other books by Alan Seale

*Intuitive Living: A Sacred Path*
*Soul Mission, Life Vision*
*The Manifestation Wheel: A Practical Process for Creating Miracles*

LaVergne, TN USA
29 September 2010
199028LV00001B/52/P